P9-DFX-074

Farrar Straus Giroux Books for Young Readers
175 Fifth Avenue, New York 10010

Lizzie Murphy photograph courtesy of the National Baseball Hall of Fame.

Copyright © 2015 by Emily Arnold McCully
Color separations by Bright Arts (H.K.) Ltd.
Printed in China by Toppan Leefung Printing Ltd.,
Dongguan City, Guangdong Province
Designed by Roberta Pressel
First edition, 2015
1   3   5   7   9   10   8   6   4   2

mackids.com

Library of Congress Cataloging-in-Publication Data
McCully, Emily Arnold.
    Queen of the diamond : the Lizzie Murphy story / Emily Arnold McCully.
        pages cm
    Summary: "A picture book biography about Lizzie Murphy, the first woman
to play in a major league exhibition game and the first person to play on
both the New England and American leagues' all-star teams"—Provided by
publisher.
    ISBN 978-0-374-30007-4 (hardback)
    1. Murphy, Lizzie, 1894–1964. 2. Baseball players—United States—
Biography. 3. Baseball players—United States—Biography—Pictorial
works. 4. Women baseball players—United States—Biography. 5. Women
baseball players—United States—Biography—Pictorial works. I. Title.

GV865.M795M33 2015
796.357092—dc23
[B]
                                                                    2014010987

Farrar Straus Giroux Books for Young Readers may be purchased for business
or promotional use. For information on bulk purchases please contact
Macmillan Corporate and Premium Sales Department at (800) 221-7945 x5442
or by email at specialmarkets@macmillan.com.

For Karen Romer—thanks for telling me about Lizzie
—E.A.M.

In 1900, baseball was America's national pastime. No other form of entertainment came close. Every boy owned a ball, a glove, and a dream.

In Warren, Rhode Island, there were several amateur teams and Lizzie Murphy followed all of them. Her father had played on one as a young man. Her brother, Henry, was a shortstop on one of the best boys' teams. To sharpen his game, he played catch with Lizzie.

Even at six years old, Lizzie threw straight to Henry's glove.
Thunk! Thunk! Thunk! They did this for hours, until the sun went
down and the fireflies winked.

"You're a natural, Lizzie," her father said.

"I want to be a first baseman like you were," Lizzie told him.

"She's good enough," Henry said.

"Don't encourage her," said her mother. "It's not a game for girls."

"But she loves it," her father said. "She can throw and catch as well as any boy." He gave Lizzie his old ball and glove to keep. She carried them everywhere.

Lizzie went to all of Henry's games. She watched the plays and could see that a fielder had to throw fast and true to the baseman for an out. She was dying to be on the field.

When she was eight, she asked Eddie, the captain, to let her try out for the team. He shook his head no.

"Please?" Lizzie begged.

"You're a girl, Lizzie!"

"She's good," Henry said. "She can help us win."

The boys laughed.

Lizzie saw they wouldn't budge. "Then can I carry your bats?" she asked.

A girl batboy? The team huddled for a minute.

"Okay, sure," Eddie said, sighing.

It was a start. She was part of the team.

A few weeks later, they went to nearby Cranston to play another team.

"Who has the ball?" Eddie asked when they got there. Everyone looked sheepish. No one on either team had brought one.

"What do we do? It's time to start."

"I've got a ball," Lizzie piped up.

"Good," Eddie said. "Let's have it."

Lizzie held on to it. "I want to play first base," she said.

There was dead silence.

"Let her play!" Henry said.

Eddie rolled his eyes and waved Lizzie to first base. She couldn't help grinning.

The Cranston team started hooting and calling out insults.

"Go back to your knitting."

"Where is your dolly?"

Lizzie punched her glove. She had a job to do. She looked over at Henry to see if he was ready. Henry nodded. The third baseman nodded. Next, she checked the pitcher, Mick. He was watching the catcher for a signal. Then he glanced at Lizzie. He raised an eyebrow. She punched her glove.

Okay, let's go, let's go. You can do it, she muttered to herself.

The first batter stepped up to the plate. Mick threw the pitch. A strike. He wound up and threw again.

CRACK!

It was a grounder to Henry. He scooped up the ball and fired it to Lizzie the way they'd practiced for years. She caught it. The runner was out.

At bat, Lizzie hit two doubles, a triple, and then a single.
Once, she struck out. But that happened in the ninth inning and
her team was already ahead 10–0. Lizzie tingled with happiness.

"Lizzie, you can play with us any time you want," said Eddie.
The other players called out, "Three cheers for Lizzie!"
Henry pretended to sock her.

When Lizzie turned twelve, she went to work in the
textile mill with the rest of the Murphys. Standing at a loom
all day, she had plenty of time to daydream. Memories of
base hits, double plays, the thrill of fast teamwork.

On her off days, during the cold months, she practiced the violin,

played on ice hockey teams, and won foot races.

Lizzie was an all-around athlete with a lot of talent. In the warm months, she won quite a few swimming races, too. But she always ended up on a baseball diamond.

By the time she was fifteen, she was a regular on two amateur teams, the
Silk Hats and the Warren Baseball Club. She played any position that was open
because she was equally good at them all.

Three years later, her mother sat her down for a serious talk.

"You are a grown-up lady now, Lizzie."

Lizzie figured she knew what was coming.

"It's time to give up baseball."

"But it's what I do best."

"A woman can't support herself on a ball field. It's hard enough for a man."

Maybe her mother was right, she thought. Baseball wasn't for girls.

The next day, Lizzie watched a game instead of playing in one.
It was strange to sit in the stands. In the fourth inning, a batter hit
a weak ball to the third baseman, who dropped it. Lizzie leaped to
her feet and nearly ran out onto the field. She loved baseball! She
was better than most of the men! How could she give it up?

Warren also had a semipro team, and the players were paid. Maybe she could make a living at baseball. She had to try! The manager had seen her play.

"Sure, we'll start you at first base," he said. His eyes twinkled. He was thinking that people would come in droves to see a girl on the field.

The newspaper printed the story: Lizzie Murphy had signed with the team.

"This is just the beginning," Lizzie told her parents. "I'll be traveling all over. It will be an education!"

"How will you ever get married?" her mother said.

"Don't care. I want to play baseball."

The stands were already overflowing with excited
fans when Lizzie arrived for her first game.
"Wow!" Lizzie said. "What's going on?"
"They're here to see you," said the manager.

Lizzie trotted to first base, telling herself to calm down.
Let's go. You're playing your favorite position. Way to go! She
punched her glove and bounced on her toes.

Then the announcer yelled, *"PLAY BALL!"*

The first batter popped up to the shortstop. The second hit a grounder to the second baseman, who pegged it to Lizzie, who tagged the batter out. And the third struck out. Inning over. When Lizzie was up, she hit a triple.

Her team won, 10–2. Lizzie was mobbed.

When the manager handed out pay envelopes to the players, he walked right past Lizzie.

Lizzie kept quiet, but she made a plan. At practice the next week she gave it her all. On Saturday they were to play a game in Newport. Lizzie waited until everyone else had boarded the bus. Then she refused to get on.

"Lizzie, let's go!" barked the manager. "We'll be late."

"You owe me my cut from last week's game," said Lizzie. "The men got five dollars and a share of what the fans dropped in the can you passed around the bleachers."

"Look here, Lizzie," the manager said. "You'll quit to get married someday. These fellows have to earn a living."

"I do, too!" Lizzie protested. "This is my job."

"People are coming just to watch you!" the manager sputtered.

"That's right!" said Lizzie. "Pay me the same as the men."

Players called from the bus. "Hey, she earned it, fair and square."

"Give Lizzie her share."

"Hand it over."

"Good for you, Lizzie."

The manager handed her five dollars plus her share of what they'd collected from fans.

Lizzie boarded the bus.

"Hip-hip-hooray for Lizzie Murphy!" the team cried.

A few days later, Lizzie's mother gave her a package. It was her baseball uniform, washed and neatly folded. Across the chest and the back, her mother had stitched the words **LIZZIE MURPHY**.

"You're a pro now," said her mother. "Your fans will want to see your name."

For the next seventeen years, Lizzie Murphy played professional baseball. And she always made sure she was paid as much as the men.

Fans called her the Queen of Baseball.

Author's Note

Women playing baseball paralleled the burgeoning campaign for women's suffrage. First, there were teams formed at the new women's colleges after the Civil War. Fitness, exercise, and personal freedom were emphasized. Later, semiprofessional and professional teams followed. For a time, teams were called Bloomers, after the revival of the loose trousers worn by the players. Women who earned their living from baseball and who played with and against men had to be highly skilled. They were always a big draw.

Lizzie Murphy's (1894–1964) superb record over three summers on her Warren semipro team led to a contract with the Providence Independents, who played all over New England and eastern Canada. Lizzie had herself listed in the telephone book as "Lizzie Murphy, ballplayer."

Next, she won a contract with the Boston All-Stars. The manager told reporters, "She swells attendance, and she's worth every cent I pay her. But, most important, she produces the goods."

Lizzie's pay was the same as the men's, but that wasn't much. To supplement her income, she had cards printed up with her picture and statistics and sold them to fans between innings. Sometimes this sideline brought in fifty dollars per game.

Lizzie Murphy was the first woman to play in a major league exhibition game and the first person to play on the National and the American leagues' all-star teams. In one exhibition game, she faced the great pitcher Satchel Paige. If anyone expected Paige to soften his pitches for a woman, they were wrong. He bore down with everything he had. Nevertheless, Lizzie hit a single off him!

Lizzie Murphy played professional baseball from 1918 to 1935. When she retired, she still had to earn a living. Even with the income from her baseball cards, she hadn't been able to save much money. She cleaned houses, went back to the textile mill, and harvested quahogs and other clams. She got married, too.

Sources

Berlage, Gai Ingham. *Women in Baseball: The Forgotten History*. Westport, Conn.: Praeger Publishers, 1994.

Gregorich, Barbara. *Women at Play: The Story of Women in Baseball*. San Diego, Calif.: Harcourt Brace & Company, 1993.

sportsillustrated.cnn.com/vault/article/magazine/MAG1077366/3/index.htm

www.exploratorium.edu/baseball/murphy.html